GEMS
of the Golden State

The 15 best CAVES to visit in California

Photographed by Peter and Ann Bosted   Written by Ann Bosted

Copyright © 2003 by Ann Bosted

Photographs © 2003 by Peter and Ann Bosted
Map of California Cavern © 2003 by Peter Bosted
Map of Crystal Cave © 2003 by Peter and Ann Bosted
Map of Lake Shasta Caverns © 2003 by Mike and Lynne Sims
Map of Mercer Caverns © 2003 by Bruce Rogers
Map of Mitchell Caverns © 2003 by Bob Richards

All rights reserved, including the right to
reproduce this work in any form
whatsoever without permission in writing
from the publisher, except for brief
passages in connection with a review.

For information write:

The Donning Company Publishers
184 Business Park Drive, Suite 206
Virginia Beach, VA 23462

Barbara Bolton, Project Director
Steve Mull, General Manager
Barbara Buchanan, Office Manager
Scott Rule, Designer
Mary Ellen Wheeler, Proofreader

ISBN 1-57864-235-3
Cataloging-in-Publication Data
Available upon request.

Printed in the United States of America

CONTENTS

GEMS

of the Golden State

Lava Beds
(pg. 50)

Pluto's Cave
(pg. 58)

Lake Shasta Caverns
(pg. 32)

Redding Subway Cave
(pg. 57)

Kok-chee-shup-chee
(pg. 31)

Black Chasm
(pg. 12)

Sacramento

California Cavern
(pg. 20)

Mercer
Caverns
(pg. 38)

Stockton

San Francisco

Modesto

Moaning Cavern
(pg. 46)

Natural Bridges
(pg. 19)

Fresno

Boyden Cavern
(pg. 16)

Balconies Cave
(pg. 60)

Crystal Cave (pg. 26)

Bakersfield

Mitchell Caverns
(pg. 42)

Los Angeles

The 15 best CAVES to visit in California

Sunny Jim Cave
(pg.59)

San Diego

3

Tom's Lake, California Cavern

AUTHOR'S NOTE

I feel fortunate to provide the text for a book whose subject has been an enjoyable part of my life since I first shone my headlamp into a California cave and learned the thrill of discovering the underground. Researching this guide has helped me learn more about the caves I thought I knew so well.

My husband, Peter, has been an invaluable support in this project. We have been photographing caves since 1982 and this book is illustrated with some of our photos. Photography in complete darkness is tricky. Generally, Peter frames the photo and calculates the exposure and focus, while I set out as many of our lightweight electronic strobes as needed. Many of our friends help us by modeling or holding strobes. The photo on the opposite page required seven strobes and four assistants.

To make our photos more easily understood we often use people for scale. We received special permission from the caves' owners or managers to allow our models, all experienced cavers, to carefully leave the trail for a few photos in this book. Please do not be misled into thinking all visitors may do the same.

California has a tremendous variety of caves. I obviously chose all the caves that offer guided tours on a regular basis, to which I added some of the better self-guiding ones. I avoided caves with obvious dangers or that required special vehicles to get there.

While I have made every effort to include up-to-date information, I strongly advise readers to telephone ahead for the latest information before visiting a cave offering guided tours. Those intending to do the self-guiding tours must acquire suitable equipment, such as helmets, lights, boots, and clothing. Please, never cave alone!

Most of the caves in this book have been millions of years in the making. I trust that all readers appreciate how privileged we all are to enjoy these unique natural wonders. Today's cave explorers are responsible for preserving the caves for future visitors.

Cave softly,

Ann Bosted
Menlo Park, California.
www.cavepics.com

Paleo-Indians, while migrating from Alaska to South America ten thousand to fifteen thousand years ago, likely used some California caves. Some twelve-thousand-year-old tools have been found in Daisy Cave on the Channel Islands. Radiocarbon dates confirm that Indians used many of the Mother Lode caves as burial caves between two thousand and twenty-five hundred years ago. Indians also left petroglyphs in lava tubes, possibly for ceremonial reasons.

"Gold Fever" began in 1848 when gold was found near Coloma. The Golden State swarmed with prospectors. They explored the Mother Lode, discovering California Cavern, Calaveras Natural Bridges, and Bower Cave in about 1850, Moaning Cavern in 1851, Black Chasm in 1854, and Mercer Caverns in 1885. Silver miners found Mitchell Caverns in the early 1860's and loggers discovered Boyden Cavern in 1888.

In 1852, near Weaverville in Northern California, a posse massacred a group of Indians near Kok-Chee-Shup-Chee (Natural Bridge). A rancher found Pluto's Cave near Weed in 1863, and Indians led settlers to Lake Shasta Caverns in 1877.

Development of these natural wonders soon followed. In 1851 a hotel was built for California Cavern's tourists and in 1856 Bower Cave was used as a ballroom. From about 1875 Calaveras Natural Bridges was a popular weekend picnic resort. Tours of Mercer Caverns began in 1885.

These Victorian tourists were in awe of caves. They lived in an unhurried age, when two days' travel by horse to visit a cave was considered time well spent. By the dim light of candles they explored unimaginable sights. In detailed, fanciful prose, they invariably exaggerated their adventures. They often left their names ornately and meticulously carved into the cave walls. John Muir, a prolific nature writer and founder of the Sierra Club, visited Bower Cave in 1874, California Cavern in 1876, and Pluto's Cave and Lava Beds in 1888.

Most of California's show caves opened for business during the twentieth century. Sunny Jim Cave admitted tourists in 1902 and Moaning Cavern opened in 1922. The stock market collapse in 1929 resulted in the Great Depression and the founding of the Civilian Conservation Corps (CCC) that developed Crystal Cave, Lava Beds, Balconies Cave, and Boyden Cavern. The distinctive Spider Web Gate at Crystal Cave is a monument to this period.

The hippie movement began in the 1960's as the baby-boomers came of age. This mobile, well-educated, freedom-loving generation, which grew up vacationing along established tourist routes in their parents' station wagons, craved adventure. Backpackers invaded the Sierra and Yosemite became a rock climbers' mecca. Caving grew in popularity and clubs were organized for recreational exploration and study of caves. Most of the caves in this book have been surveyed and mapped since the 1970's.

Since the 1980's, off-trail caving tours have been offered at California Cavern, Crystal Cave, Moaning Cavern; and, for a while, at Black Chasm, Lake Shasta Caverns, and Mercer Caverns.

GEOLOGY IN CARBONATE CAVES

The story of California caves is long and complicated, stretching back 250 million years to the earth's most recent super-continent, Pangea, when only small sea creatures inhabited its shores. As these animals died, their skeletons sank to the bottom of the adjacent seas. Over about 50 million years the calcium carbonate in the skeletons accumulated in layers thick enough to form limestone.

About 200 million years ago, Pangea broke up and continental plates began moving apart in a process called "Plate Tectonics." The layers of limestone which today host Mitchell Caverns were deposited on the North American Plate. In contrast, the rock of the Sierra Nevada, Mother Lode, and Lake Shasta areas, formed on the Pacific Plate, possibly as reefs.

About 120 million years ago, the North American Plate overrode the Pacific Plate, scraping rocks off its surface as you would use a shovel to scoop up dirt clods from a driveway. While being "shoveled" from one plate to another, the layers of limestone in the present-day Sierra and Mother Lode were broken up, squeezed, and buried so they became changed, or "metamorphosed," into marble. This can be compared to making mashed potatoes — the more you cook and mash them, the more they metamorphose. In contrast, the limestone around Lake Shasta was also "shoveled," but barely metamorphosed, and its fossils are still preserved. Experts have recognized fusulinids, brachiopods (lamp shells), bryozoans (sea fans), mollusks (snails and clams), and a large variety of corals. By 80 million years ago, the metamorphosis was complete.

About ten million years ago, the Sierra Nevada was uplifted about seven thousand to eight thousand feet. Stress-induced cracks developed parallel to the crest of the Sierra — the same orientation as Crystal Cave and Boyden Cavern. Carbonate rocks (limestone and marble) are "soluble,"

SUMMARY	LAKE SHASTA AREA	MOTHER LODE AREA	HIGH SIERRA	MOJAVE DESERT
ACCRETED TERRANES?	YES - LIKELY FROM VOLCANIC ISLAND REEFS	YES - FROM CONTINENTAL MARGIN BASINS & ISLANDS		NO
FORMATION	MCCLOUD LIMESTONE	CALAVERAS GROUP OF THE WESTERN METAMORPHIC BELT	BOYDEN CAVE PENDANT & SEQUOIA ROOF PENDANT	BIRD SPRINGS FORMATION
FOSSILS	ABUNDANT CORALS & FUSULINID FORAMINIFERA	BADLY PRESERVED SOLITARY CORALS, FUSULINID FORAMINIFERA	CEPHALAPODS, SEA LILIES	CORALS, LAMP SHELLS, ALGAE, WORM BURROWS
AGE	EARLY PERMIAN	PENNSYLVANIAN TO PERMIAN	PENNSYLVANIAN TO TRIASSIC	MIDDLE TO LATE PENNSYLVANIAN
METAMOR- PHOSED?	NO - LIMESTONE	YES - MARBLE	YES - MARBLE	NO - LIMESTONE

which means that acid can dissolve holes in them. In nature, water from rain and snow dissolves carbon dioxide in the air and soil to form carbonic acid. When this enters the cracks and crevices of soluble carbonate rocks, the cracks slowly get bigger and caves develop.

Many of the caves in California have formed in the past three million years. Some Mother Lode caves began forming about 1.6 million years ago, Boyden about 1.4 million years ago, and Crystal over a million years ago.

Typically, caves form at the water table, so a slowly dropping water table will generally result in huge cave chambers. However, with the rapid uplift of the Sierra Nevada, the rivers have cut steep canyons, causing ground water to drain relatively quickly from the caves, leaving behind tall, narrow passages and chambers. As new, deeper caves and passages form, the older and higher ones stop growing. For example, water has drained from Lake Shasta, Mercer, Mitchell, and most of Moaning. Boyden, Crystal, and Natural Bridge still have active streams flowing through their lower passages and the water table is seen at the bottom of Black Chasm. California Cavern is so close to the water table that it floods each winter.

(Opposite) A Horn Coral at the entrance of Lake Shasta Caverns

(Below) Flooded tourist trail in California Cavern

9

SPELEOTHEMS IN CARBONATE CAVES

California's carbonate caves are well decorated with mineral deposits called speleothems. Rain or melting snow dissolves carbon dioxide in the soil and air to form a weak carbonic acid. This seeps through cracks in the rocks and dissolves microscopic amounts of the limestone or marble. Calcite speleothems are formed when this mixture enters the cave chamber (as a drip or under pressure) and carbon dioxide is released. Calcite can no longer be held in solution and is deposited.

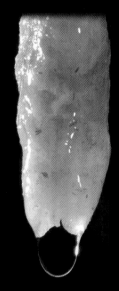

Stalactites grow down, like icicles, from dripping cracks in the cave's ceiling. Crystals grow from their tips and their sides, so some are long and thin like carrots, while others are quite broad.

Stalagmites grow on the floor or ledges beneath drips. Crystal layers form on their tips and sides, so they can look like broomsticks or cones.

Memory crutch: Notice that Stalactite has a "c" for ceiling, and it hangs "tite." Stalagmite has a "g" for ground and "mite" get up there.

Columns form when a stalagmite and a stalactite grow together. Columns thicken with age.

Flowstone grows when water flows over rocks and other speleothems creating a fairly smooth surface.

This sectioned stalagmite clearly shows the growth rings over thousands of years. The stalagmite on the left grew around the older one on the right. Both were coated with more growth on the front to make one huge speleothem.

Soda straws are thin, hollow, and grow down from ceilings or other speleothems. Water moves down the center of the "straw," so it grows only from its tip. See page 23.

Drapes, curtains, or bacon grow along sloping ceilings when water trickles along the slope, depositing crystals in thin bands, often of different hues. Growth takes place on their lower edges. See pages 18, 28, 34, 41, and back cover.

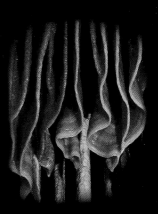

Helictites grow from water that is under pressure. Since the water is forced out of cracks, crystals can grow on any surface. Any shape is possible. See pages 14 and 15.

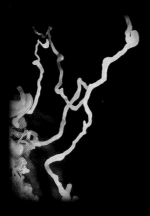

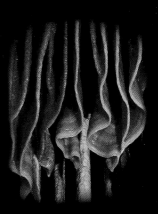

Crystals usually grow around the edges of shallow pools as the water evaporates. They are easily observed when the pool is dry. See pages 26 and 36.

Shields grow from water under pressure. In this case the water is forced out of a crack in a spray, so the shield resembles a flat, circular disk with crystal growth along its outer edges. See page 45.

Speleothem growth is uneven, as demonstrated by the depostis on this iron ladder that has been under dripping water for about fifty years. The right side has about four inches of growth, while the left side, a foot away, has about one inch.

11

Black Chasm is the only cave in the state to be accorded the coveted National Natural Landmark status, chiefly for its spectacular display of helictites, which are certainly the best in California.

HISTORY

Gold miners found the cave in about 1851. In 1854 the first rope descent was witnessed by E. Sammis, who wrote:

"Several pounds of candles were taken along and placed in the soft clay, which formed the sloping floor of the cavern. The advance man of the party, not having a realizing sense of the abyss yawning below him, stood without fear on the steep slope, where a slip of the foot would have sent him sliding to the bottom. As the descent progressed and the cave became lighted up, a vaulted chamber, large enough to contain the largest trees, came into view. Stalactites sparkled like diamonds all over the roof."

A miner, who built redwood decking into the first room, gave walking tours into Black Chasm in the 1860's. This structure eventually collapsed.

Scuba divers from San Francisco explored the lakes at the bottom of the cave in 1961 and 1962. Tom Rohrer drew a preliminary map and the group installed a manhole cover over the upper entrance.

Cave accidents in California are rare, but in May, 1974, a twenty-three-year-old inexperienced caver from Sacramento, accidentally dropped his flashlight at the entrance. As he reached down into the cave to retrieve it, he lost his balance and fell 174 feet. He survived, but his back was broken. A large team took about twenty hours to rescue him.

Cavers recommended the cave for National Natural Landmark status in 1970, which was granted in 1976. In 1986 Peter Bosted led the survey of 1,815 feet of this complicated, three-dimensional cave and drew a map.

In 1996 the Fairchild family's corporation (operator of Boyden Cavern, California Cavern, and Moaning Cavern) bought the land around the cave and offered "wild" tours. In November, 1999, electricity was brought to the cave. Steve Fairchild invited Peter Bosted, Glen Malliet, and me to help him install the first electric lights in the cave. We were all amazed to see the cave lit to a magnificence well beyond the capability of our meager headlamps.

In June, 2000, Fairchild led the construction of an elevated walkway using modern, long-lasting materials. Tours to the *Landmark Room* began in May 2001, and the Visitor Center opened in the fall of 2003. The cave is presently being resurveyed to include changes and recent discoveries.

THE TOUR

The tour is short but varied, encompassing the historic, the huge, and the beautiful, all without touching the ground. The tour begins in the *Historic Chamber*, which was visited by the Victorians. The *Colossal Chamber* offers breathtaking vistas in all directions, including the surreal blue-green lake about ninety feet below. The *Landmark Room* has a mass of helictites. Among them, visitors can recognize *The Dragon*, *The Candy Cane*, and *The Reindeer*.

TO VISIT

From Jackson, proceed east on Route 88 to Pine Grove. Turn left on the Volcano-Pine Grove Road and proceed towards Volcano for 2 1/2 miles. Turn right onto the Pioneer-Volcano Road. After a few hundred yards, turn right and

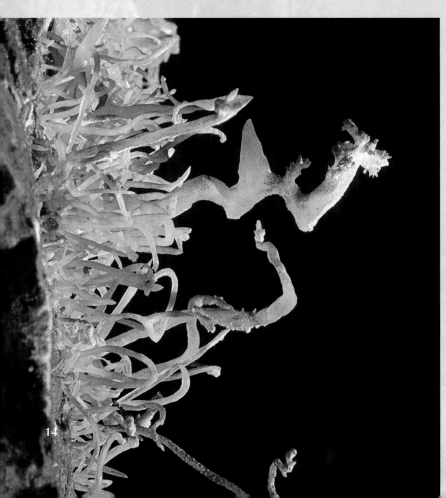

(Opposite) The Landmark Room

(Bottom left) The Dragon

(Right and below) Helictites

follow signs to the parking lot. Phone (209) 736-2708 or (866) 762-2837 from 9-5. www.caverntours.com

Cavern temperature is 58°F. Elevation is 2,250 feet. Tours last about fifty minutes.

Other attractions include the Masonic Caves in Volcano, Indian Grinding Rock State Historic Park, Daffodil Hill in the springtime, historic St. George Hotel in Volcano, and Sutter Gold Mine Tours in Sutter Creek.

The Wedding Cake

Boyden Cavern is stunningly picturesque inside and out. Located in the heart of the Sierra Nevada, the approach offers spectacular vistas of Kings Canyon. The turbulent Kings River is best viewed from the short switch-back trail to the cave entrance, about one hundred and twenty-five feet above the river. Once inside, the tall, spacious cave is profusely decorated with a variety of large speleothems. The main cave passage parallels the crest of the Sierra and penetrates the mountain for about nine hundred feet.

HISTORY

A logger, writer, prospector and mountaineer, "Put" Boyden is credited with discovering the cave in 1908, but it seems likely that loggers first found it about 1888. Boyden, with his partner and grubstaker Denver Church, placed a mining claim on the area, but cave exploration soon became their chief interest. They established a camp about a quarter-mile downstream from the cave and built a heavy wooden gate over the cave entrance. In 1916, when Boyden died from hypothermia in the canyon, Church's interests shifted away from caves as he became a con-gressman and then a judge in Fresno. He let his mining claim lapse in the hope that the federal government would preserve Boyden Cavern by including it in the National Park.

In 1923 Robert C. Middleton, a journalist for the Fresno Morning Republican and a member of a major, week-long expedition to the caves of Windy Gulch, wrote: "Skirting the stream, the visitors walked down a corridor the like of which man has never been able to reproduce on top of the earth. Stalactites and stalag-mites in profusion began to push themselves into view in a striking panorama, restricted only by the gleam of the electric torches. Boyden is both austere and beautiful."

In 1939 the Civilian Conservation Corps (CCC) completed Highway 180 past the cave and installed trails in the cave and a platform at the cave's entrance. In 1942 the gate was built; and in 1951, after electric lights were installed, public tours were allowed in the cave. That year a group of cavers from Los Angeles dug into "new" passage.

The Drapery Room

THE TOUR

The tour begins in a spacious chamber, goes on to *The Pancake Room*, named for a huge formation that resembles a stack of pancakes, complete with dripping syrup and a pat of butter. Then comes *The Inspiration Grotto*, the *Crystal Cascade*, *Fat Man's Misery*, *The Wedding Cake*, and *The Drapery Room* with *The Christmas Tree*. From the *River Room*, the route drops down to the stream, which it follows to the lower entrance.

TO VISIT

From Fresno, follow Route 180 through Grant Grove and and then for nineteen miles toward Cedar Grove. The cave is open from about May to October, depending on snowfall. Phone: (209) 736-2708 or (866) 762-2837 from 9-5. www.caverntours.com

Cavern temperature is 55°F. Elevation is 3,063 feet. Tours last about one hour.

Other attractions include backpacking and hiking trails from Cedar Grove, the *General Grant Tree*, and Crystal Cave (pg. 26).

CALAVERAS NATURAL BRIDGES

Gold miners discovered The Calaveras Natural Bridges in about 1849. One famous chronicler of the time, J. D. Borthwick, wrote, "In any part of the Old World such a place would be made the object of a pilgrimage."

TO VISIT

The sign to the caves is on the Parrots Ferry Road between Vallecito and Columbia, about two miles downhill from the Moaning Cave turnoff. Park on a stretch of abandoned road. The trail down to the caves begins at the gate and takes about twenty minutes.

"The Bridges" (really travertine caves) became a popular picnic resort in the 1880's, run by a colorful Gold Rush character, Lorenzo Anson Barnes, who entertained his visitors with stories of his adventures. At that time the stream was diverted to one side so up to one hundred people could picnic in the cave. In 2003 Dave Bunnell surveyed the upper bridge to 250 feet and the lower one to 180 feet.

The upper "bridge" is well decorated with flowstone. Its floor is now a single large, deep pool kept chilly by spring water. The lower "bridge" is located about half a mile downstream. This is a delightful place to picnic and swim in the hot summer months. For safety and comfort, bring an inflatable air mattress or inner tube.

The Jungle Room

Of all the caves described in this book, California Cavern has the greatest extent of passages and chambers open to the public. Each year many thousands of visitors enjoy the longest and most varied of any cavern tour offered in the state, called *The Trail of Lights*.

HISTORY

In about 1850 a gold miner named Captain Taylor discovered a small hole in the rock that was blowing cold air. He enlarged it so that he could crawl through. After about thirty feet he discovered the huge rooms that inspired one of its first names "Mammoth Cave."

It became the first show cave in the state when, in about 1851, W. McGee and Henry Angell claimed the cave and erected a hotel near its entrance at a cost of $4,500. They enlarged the entrance and constructed wooden walkways to keep tourists out of the mud. Several names were used for the cave in various journals, newspapers, and maps, but all writers described the cave using superlatives. Hundreds of visitors carved their names into the rock walls (See page 6). A mining camp, called Cave City, grew around the cavern.

By 1860 the Gold Rush had slowed, and by the mid-1860's the town had dwindled to a third of its former size. In 1876, when John Muir visited the cave then known as Cave City Cave, only the home of the cave's caretakers remained. Muir wrote:

"We were shown a large room that was occasionally used as a dancing hall; another that was used as a chapel, with natural pulpit and crosses and pews, sermons in every stone, where a priest said mass. It was delightful to witness here the infinite deliberation of Nature, and the simplicity of her methods in the production of such mighty results, such perfect repose combined with restless enthusiastic energy. The archways and ceilings were everywhere hung with down-growing crystals, like inverted groves of leafless saplings, some of them large, others delicately attenuated, each tipped with a single drop of water. The only appreciable sounds were the dripping and tinkling of water falling into pools or faintly splashing on the crystal floors."

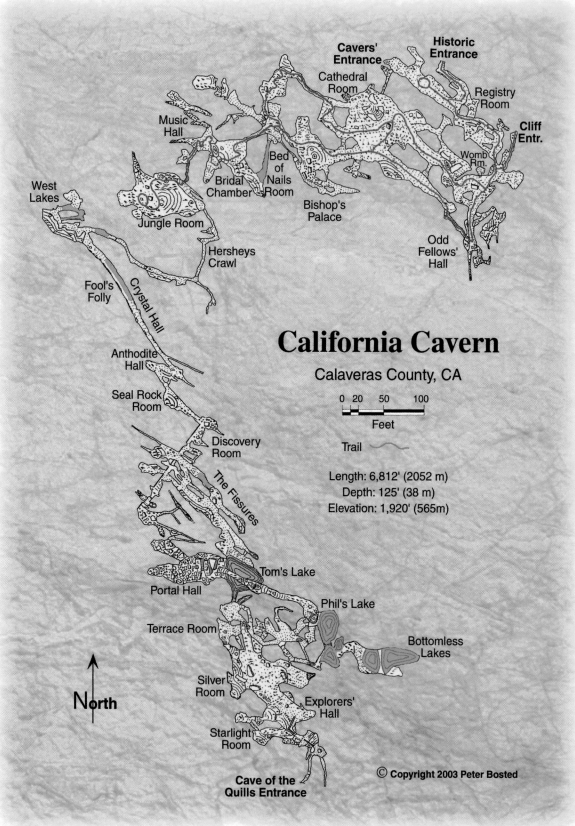

Cavers' Entrance

Historic Entrance

Cathedral Room

Registry Room

Cliff Entr.

Music Hall

Womb Rm.

Bridal Chamber

Bed of Nails Room

Bishop's Palace

West Lakes

Jungle Room

Hersheys Crawl

Odd Fellows' Hall

Fool's Folly

Crystal Hall

Anthodite Hall

Seal Rock Room

Discovery Room

The Fissures

California Cavern

Calaveras County, CA

```
0   20   50        100
```
Feet

Trail

Length: 6,812' (2052 m)
Depth: 125' (38 m)
Elevation: 1,920' (565m)

Tom's Lake

Phil's Lake

Portal Hall

Terrace Room

Bottomless Lakes

North

Silver Room

Explorers' Hall

Starlight Room

Cave of the Quills Entrance

© Copyright 2003 Peter Bosted

In October, 1960, a caver and cave scientist, Tom Aley, was hired by the landowners to explore the cave. He squeezed through a very tight, awkward crawl near *The Bridal Chamber* to discover *The Jungle Room.* Today this is the destination of *The Trail of Lights* tour. Aley reported his find to his employers, but protected this pristine room by keeping it secret for twenty years.

John and Steve Fairchild, whose family's corporation operated Moaning and Boyden Caverns, bought Cave City Cave and Quill in 1980. They outbid a real estate developer who would have closed the cave and subdivided the property. They enlarged passageways to accommodate tours and installed trails and lights. The cave became known as California Cavern and in 1983 was awarded State Historic Landmark status.

Stalactites and soda straws look like a jungle

The Bridal Veil

TO VISIT

From San Andreas go east on Mountain Ranch Road for about nine miles. Turn right at the Historic Landmark sign. Turn left at the T-junction and follow the signs to the cave (about two miles). Phone: (209) 736-2708 or (866) 762-2837 from 9-5. www.caverntours.com

Cavern temperature is 55°F. Elevation is 1,650 feet. *The Trail of Lights* tour takes about an hour.

Other attractions include the historic towns of San Andreas, Angels Camp, and Jamestown. Black Chasm (pg. 12) is nearby.

CALIFORNIA CAVERN CAVING TRIPS

No words or photos can adequately capture the sheer fun of a caving expedition in California Cavern. For visitors who have never tried caving with only a headlamp for light, this is an unparalleled opportunity. Cavers are provided with a helmet, light, coveralls, gloves, and an experienced guide. They have a choice between two expeditions.

The Mammoth Expedition takes two to three hours and is suitable for the whole family, including children over eight years old. Cavers enter the historic section of the cave by way of a climb-down entrance dubbed *The Meat Grinder*. From there they explore some of the small, interesting passages and rooms off the *Trail of Lights* tour. These have apt names like *The Womb Room*, *Worm Squirm*, *Deadman's Hole*, and *Pancake Crawl*.

For the more adventurous, there is *The Middle Earth Expedition* that takes four to five hours and includes highlights of *The Mammoth Expedition* and a route through the muddiest part of the cave where passages have names like *Fool's Folly* (see map on page 22). The highlight is a raft ride across surreal *Tom's Lake*. To get from *Explorers' Hall* to the *Quill* entrance involves climbing a steep ladder. Cavers emerge muddy, tired, and happy. Outstanding speleothems can be seen all along the route.

The Womb Room

HISTORY

The Middle Earth route is the result of a series of discoveries by several cave explorers. In the spring of 1960 two scientist cavers from UC Berkeley, Tom Aley and Howard Sturgis, found another cave near the historic entrance to Cave City Cave. They named it Cave of the Quills for the profusion of porcupine quills and because Sturgis encountered a porcupine while digging his way into a small chamber. Aley and Sturgis descended a twenty-foot drop. The following weekend, Aley returned with Art Lange and Kathy Connell. They descended a fifty-foot drop over glistening flowstone to a huge chamber they named

Explorers' Hall. At that time the cave was partly flooded, but later in that year they found *Tom's Lake*, which they crossed to *Portal Hall.* The following weekend Aley gated the cave. In the mid-1960's, San Francisco cavers installed the gate that is in use today.

The Middle Earth section was discovered from both ends. In 1979 Steve Fairchild, Jr. noticed a strong wind coming out of a hole in the floor of *The Jungle Room.* That led to the discovery of *Hershey Crawl*, now enlarged. It was named for the ubiquitous chocolate-like mud. When the Fairchilds bought Cave City and Quill in 1980, "ecotourism" and "adventure travel" were in demand. The Fairchilds decided not to develop Quill, but instead to offer *Spelunker Trips* into the cave. It was on one of these, in 1980, when the Fairchilds and a client, Cheryl Freeman, dug through a constriction in *The Iron Curtain* and discovered the connection to *Hershey Crawl.* Cheryl named it *Middle Earth* from Tolkien's *The Hobbit.*

Later that year, Peter Bosted led eighteen survey trips to map the entire cave. The surveyors had to develop special techniques for working in muddy conditions. In 1984 he won a cave cartography award for his map. A simplified version is on page 22.

Tom's Lake

The Fairy Pool

26

Beneath the land of the towering giant sequoia trees is a hidden gem — beautiful Crystal Cave. It has a flowing stream, a huge chamber, and a more complicated configuration of passages than any other cave in this book.

HISTORY

In April, 1918, two park employees found the cave entrance, prompting a visit by the park superintendent, Walter Fry, and several rangers. Fry named it Crystal Cave. The cave's main passages were explored that year and the entrance was barricaded.

In 1925 Fry wrote:
"It is in this cave that nature has lavishly traced her design in decorative glory. Throughout the entire cave the calcite formations are rich and wonderfully varied in size, form and color. In some of the chambers the ceiling is a mass of stalactites, some very large, others tapering down to needlepoints. Others drop down from the roof great folds of massive draperies, while in yet others are great fluted columns of stalagmites of surpassing symmetry and beauty."

The cave was developed by members of the Civilian Conservation Corps (CCC) in1938 and 1939. The cave's famous *Spider Web Gate* was constructed from bent sections of steel bar (See photo on page 7). The cave opened for tours in May, 1940. In 1982 the Sequoia Natural History Association took over the tours.

The main passages in the cave were surveyed in the 1960's and again in 1986. In 1991 I organized a team of twenty-five cavers to survey the cave over three consecutive weekends. We discovered many rooms. A longtime caver, Brent Ort, moved some rocks and extended the northern limit of known cave to a room we named *Brent's Cavity*, because he is a dentist. The course of Pirate Creek — the water flowing through the cave from Yucca Creek to Cascade Creek — was also established.

We found and mapped 12,400 feet of passage all in a lens of marble only 700 feet long, 230 feet wide, and, except for the Oberhansly's entrance, 140 feet high. In 1993 I presented our results and map to a national caving convention where the National Caves Association

Marble Hall

*Drapes in
Marble Hall*

(see page 62) gave me an award for the best paper on a show cave. The current surveyed length is 2.95 miles.

THE TOUR

The forty-five-minute tour is limited to seventy persons. The sound of running water stays with visitors in the tall, narrow entrance passage decorated with white rimstone dams. From *The Junction Room*, the trail climbs gently through tall, narrow passages, many of which have been enlarged by blasting. *The Organ Room* is so named for a fine speleothem that resembles a pipe organ. *The Dome Room* (named by Fry) has a formation reminiscent of the Capitol dome and an unusual pool known as *The Fairy Pool*. *Fat Man's Misery* leads visitors down into *Marble Hall*, which is the largest chamber in the cave. It is about 150 feet long, 40 feet wide, and up to 60 feet high. A man-made passage leads from *Marble Hall* to the *Fault Room* and on to *Little Cathedral Room*, which has a 100-foot ceiling.

For a detailed, educational tour in a smaller group, there is the two-hour *Discovery Tour* limited to twelve people over age twelve. For the more adventurous, there is the *Wild Cave Tour*, limited to six people over

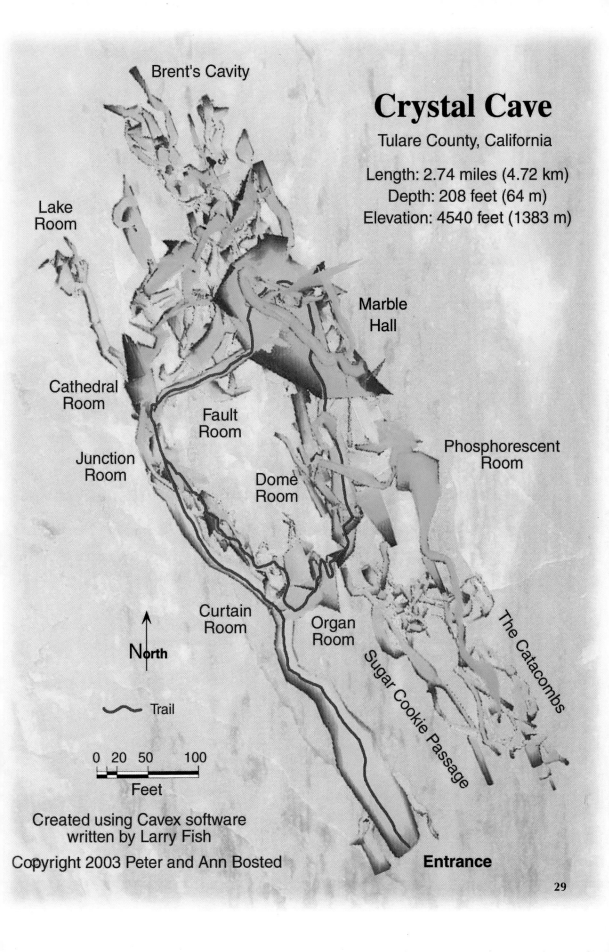

Brent's Cavity

Crystal Cave

Tulare County, California

Length: 2.74 miles (4.72 km)
Depth: 208 feet (64 m)
Elevation: 4540 feet (1383 m)

Lake
Room

Marble
Hall

Cathedral
Room

Fault
Room

Phosphorescent
Room

Junction
Room

Dome
Room

Curtain
Room

Organ
Room

North

~~~ Trail

The Catacombs

Sugar Cookie Passage

0 20 50   100

Feet

Created using Cavex software
written by Larry Fish

Copyright 2003 Peter and Ann Bosted

Entrance

age fifteen. The latter trip is off the regular tour route and involves crawling, stoop walking, and climbing. Visitors are loaned helmets, lights, and gloves. It lasts four to six hours.

TO VISIT

From southern California, enter Sequoia National Park by Route 198 from Visalia and purchase tickets at the Foothills Visitor Center. Allow at least an hour and a quarter to drive to the parking area from Foothills.

From northern and central California, drive to Fresno and enter Kings Canyon National Park on Route 180 (The Generals Highway) and purchase tickets at the Lodgepole Visitor Center. Allow at least three-quarters of an hour to drive to the parking area from Lodgepole.

It is a half-hour walk from the parking area to the cave. Phone (559) 565-3759.

www.sequoiahistory.org

Cavern temperature is 48°F. Elevation is 4,540 feet. Tours are offered from about May to October and last about forty-five minutes. Tickets must be purchased at a visitor center before driving to the cave.

Other attractions include the *General Sherman Tree*, Moro Rock, *Tunnel Log*, hiking, and backpacking.

(Above) Off trail on the Wild Cave Tour

(Below) Caving in The Rat Hole

KOK-CHEE-SHUP-CHEE
or Natural Bridge

Kok-chee-shup-chee (or Natural Bridge) is a huge tunnel cut through a marble ridge by Bridge Gulch Creek. The arch is about 200 feet long, up to 100 feet wide, and nearly 50 feet high. It is a fine spot for contemplating, hiking, exploring, or picnicking.

TO VISIT

Leave Highway 3 four miles east of Hayfork. Proceed south on Wildwood Road for five miles, then follow the Forest Service signs pointing right onto a dirt road, then left (downhill) and through the creek to the parking area.

According to a Wintu Indian myth, a mystical man was carrying a bundle of hides, when he paused at the creek to rest. The bundle rolled into the creek and was transformed into rock with the texture of hides. Kok-Chee-Shup-Chee means "Bundle of Hides."

In 1852 a Weaverville citizen, J. R. Anderson, was killed by a band of Wintu Indians. Sheriff Dixon organized a pursuit party and tracked the elusive Indians to their camp upstream from this cave. Under the cover of darkness, Dixon's party quietly surrounded the Indian encampment. Shortly after dawn, the pursuit party opened fire on the surprised Indians. Three children were the only survivors of the 150 Wintus who inhabited the camp.

The Dome Room

A tour of Lake Shasta Caverns is like being transported to another world — and it is. The tour begins with a pontoon boat ride across one of the most scenic lakes in California. The adventurous part follows with a bus ride up a steep road to the caverns. The reward is a breathtaking view of the lake and a trip through one of the most outstanding caves in the state.

HISTORY

Excavations in this cave and others in the area have revealed a rich trove of information about extinct animals, including Ground Sloths, Shrub Oxen, Short-faced Bears, and Condors. Archeologists found an eleven-thousand-year-old spear point and tools, which were left by prehistoric Indians about twenty-five hundred years ago.

The first white discoverer of the cave was James A. Richardson, who learned about it from Charles Morton, a Wintu Indian. The Wintus were a large tribe that lived along the McCloud and Sacramento Rivers. This was the only California tribe with a written language. They considered many sites, including certain caves, hills, and rock formations, to be sacred.

Richardson and Morton entered the cave on November 3, 1878, by the natural entrance. This is located above the present tour route. They explored about eight hundred feet of passage without finding the end of the cave. The party left its signatures in what is now *The Cathedral Room*. On their next visit they made it to what is now called *The Inscription Room*.

From then, until 1959, locals willing to climb over a thousand feet to the natural entrance and then negotiate the dark chambers visited the cave. From 1947 to 1959 the Odd Fellows from Redding, who installed the iron ladders seen in the cave, often used *The Cathedral Room* for meetings and initiations. During the 1950's, cavers from San Francisco mapped more than twelve hundred feet of passage.

Mrs. Grace M. Tucker, the widow of an attorney, who had a talent for brokering, became interested in preserving the cave. In 1955 she prevailed in six title suits and became the owner of the property surrounding the caverns. She then interested Roy C. Thompson in making it a show cave. His two brothers and Ray Winther

The Cathedral Room

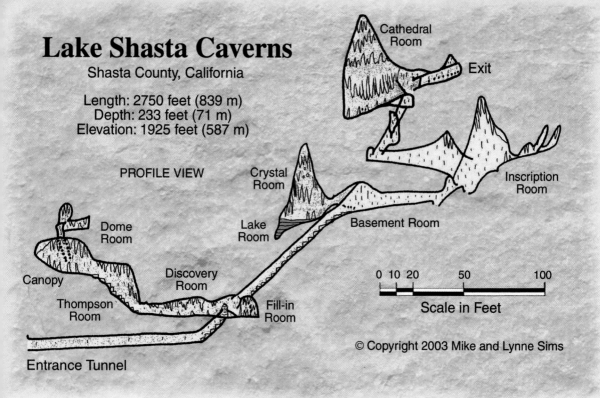

Lake Shasta Caverns

Shasta County, California

Length: 2750 feet (839 m)
Depth: 233 feet (71 m)
Elevation: 1925 feet (587 m)

PROFILE VIEW

Cathedral Room

Exit

Crystal Room

Inscription Room

Dome Room

Lake Room

Basement Room

Canopy

Discovery Room

Thompson Room

Fill-in Room

Entrance Tunnel

Scale in Feet

0 10 20   50   100

© Copyright 2003 Mike and Lynne Sims

formed a team to tackle the immense project under the name of Lake Shasta Properties, Inc. They built a road from Interstate 5 to the west side of the McCloud Arm, where the visitor center is today. They also built two docks and the facilities you see today.

The natural entrance was too high to use, so the owners bored a tunnel three hundred feet long to reach the caverns. On the way they got lucky and intersected two "virgin" rooms, which were dubbed *The Discovery Room* and *The Dome Room*.

On May 30, 1964, Lake Shasta Caverns was opened to the public. In 1972 *The Lake Room* was discovered. In 1977 a team of cavers from Oregon, led by Mike and Lynne Sims, remapped the cave. They surveyed 2,750 feet of passage and established the depth of the cave to be 233 feet. In 1985 *The Lake Room* was renamed *The Crystal Room* and opened to the public.

Crystals

36

Today about seventy-thousand people visit the caverns each year.

THE TOUR

The caverns are formed in two-hundred-million-year-old limestone, which contains many invertebrate fossils (see page 8), some of which can be seen in the rock around the entrance gate.

The cave has five levels and several large chambers. First is *The Discovery Room*, which is about two hundred feet long, fifty feet wide, and twenty to forty-five feet high. It is beautifully decorated with a plethora of wonderful speleothems. At the end of this is *The Dome Room*, which is tall, spacious, and well decorated. Stairs lead to *The Crystal Room*, which has helictites, cave coral, and bacon speleothems. In *The Inscription Room* are the names of the caverns' discoverers smoked onto the wall, and in the *Popcorn Room* is cave coral. On this tour the most spectacular room is the last — the immense *Cathedral Room*. Thanks to the electric lights, the sixty-foot-high draperies look amazing. After taking in this room, visitors emerge into the bright sunlight and descend a trail to their waiting bus.

TO VISIT

The caverns are located about sixteen miles north of Redding. From Interstate 5 take the O'Brien turn-off, and follow the signs. Phone (916) 238-2341 or (800) 795-CAVE.

www.lakeshastacaverns.com

Cavern temperature is 58°F. Elevation is 1,925 feet. The tour, including boat and bus, lasts about two hours.

Other attractions include fishing, boating, hiking, and camping around Lake Shasta; and Turtle Bay Exploration Park in Redding.

The trail from the exit to the bus

The Discovery Room

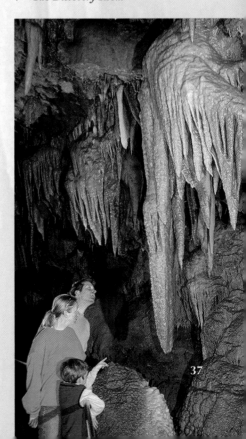

37

*Early visitors held
candles on a glim
to light their way*

38

Mercer Caverns richly deserves its title "Showplace of the Sierra." It has been a show cave longer than any other cave in California. This outstanding history of protection means that it has a lot to show.

HISTORY

Walter Mercer discovered the cave in 1885 while prospecting for gold. He found a small hole from which air was escaping, dropped a stone into the hole, and heard it bounce out of earshot. Excited by his find, he went to a nearby mine and returned with tools and candles. He enlarged the hole, lit a candle, and slid down into the cavern. Imagine his surprise and sheer wonder as he looked about him, seeing not only the wonders of nature, but also human skeletons. Afraid of a cave-in, Mercer did not linger, but left with a human thigh bone.

The next day geologist Emile Stevenot accompanied Mercer into the cave and urged him to preserve it. Within two weeks of the discovery, Prof. Henry G. Hanks, the California state mineralogist, also explored the cave and examined the human bones.

Mercer filed a mining claim on the property and purchased an additional forty acres for five dollars. He built a "hatchway" over the entrance to stop vandals from entering and began charging fifty cents for a tour of the cave. By October 18, 1885, *The Calaveras Weekly Citizen* reported:

"These night visits are quite the rage, particularly when ladies predominate the party. The cave will be one of the great attractions in the next season's tourist travel, and the hundreds who will visit will be treated to one of the greatest sights ever looked upon."

In 1886 Mercer and E.F. Floyd named many of the rooms and features in the cave and wrote a booklet titled *The New Calaveras Cave.* Electric lights were installed in 1901. The cave remained in the Mercer family until 1946 when it was sold.

In 1962 Dr. William R. Halliday wrote:

"Mercer Cave is one of the most ornate works of nature beneath the hills of the Mother Lode. Its value was recognized

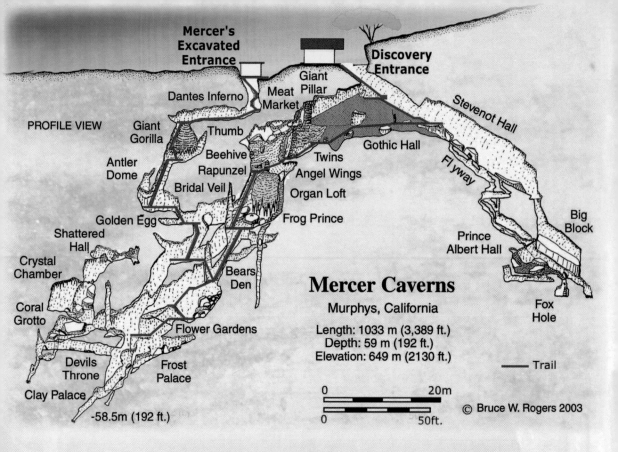

PROFILE VIEW

Mercer's Excavated Entrance

Discovery Entrance

Dantes Inferno
Meat Market
Giant Pillar
Stevenot Hall
Giant Gorilla
Thumb
Antler Dome
Beehive
Rapunzel
Bridal Veil
Twins
Angel Wings
Organ Loft
Frog Prince
Gothic Hall
Flyway
Golden Egg
Shattered Hall
Crystal Chamber
Bears Den
Prince Albert Hall
Big Block
Coral Grotto
Flower Gardens
Fox Hole
Devils Throne
Frost Palace
Clay Palace

-58.5m (192 ft.)

Mercer Caverns

Murphys, California

Length: 1033 m (3,389 ft.)
Depth: 59 m (192 ft.)
Elevation: 649 m (2130 ft.)

——— Trail

0   20m
0   50ft.

© Bruce W. Rogers 2003

The Angel Wings

at once, and the necessary steps were taken for protection against vandalism present in many nearby caves. Its speleothems probably present more variety than those of any other cave in California."

In 1985, after one hundred years operating as a show cave, the State of California designated Mercer Caverns as "Point of Historic Interest Number 004." That same year Bruce Rogers led recreational cavers from San Francisco to map the cave. He drew the profile map above, showing 3,389 feet of survey.

THE TOUR

Today the visitor sees the cave little changed from the condition Walter Mercer found it over a century ago. Tours now begin with a steep flight of stairs down to the well-decorated *Gothic Chamber*, the largest room in the cave.

At the lower end of *The Gothic Chamber* is *The Cathedral Room*. The main features are the superb *Angel Wings*, a pair of banded translucent draperies about nine feet long and three feet tall.

The tour route descends to *The Organ Loft*, which contains a formation dubbed *The Organ Pipes*, then continues down to the famed *Flower Garden*. Here a profusion of aragonite "bushes," which won the Grand Prize at the Paris World's Fair in 1900 can be seen. The bushes are composed of delicate, branching aragonite crystals, some up to three inches long. Mercer is the only California show cave with this unusual speleothem. It is thought that water entering this part of the cave is not only rich in calcium, but also in magnesium leached from the dolomitic bedrock. Chemically, aragonite is similar to calcite, but visually it is quite different. It is here that the remains of an Ice Age Sierra Ground Sloth were discovered.

Simon's Thumb

Aragonite

From this point the tour route ascends through a series of small but heavily decorated rooms to the surface.

TO VISIT

From downtown Murphys, take Sheep Ranch Road to the cave. Phone (209) 728-2101. www.mercercaverns.com

Cavern temperature is 55°F. Elevation is 2,140 feet. Tour lasts about forty-five minutes.

Other attractions include Calaveras Big Trees, The Kautz Ironstone Winery, and Moaning Cavern (page 46).

41

The Main Chamber

Mitchell Caverns are an oasis in the vast Mojave Desert. Since 1935 the beauty of these caves has provided an unexpected diversion for travelers on Interstate 40, and for those driving between Las Vegas and Los Angeles. The caverns are located in the Providence Mountains State Recreation Area, which is a very small part of the huge Mojave National Preserve.

HISTORY

Chemehuevi Indians used the caverns, perhaps as early as five hundred years ago, as evidenced by the smoke-blackened walls and hidden caches of food and tools found in the cave.

In the early 1860's silver mines were established in the immediate vicinity of the caves, which led to the growth of the town of Providence. In the early 1890's the silver market collapsed and many mines were abandoned. By 1893 Providence was a ghost town.

"Providence Caves" or "Crystal Caves" (as they were known then) saw few visitors until 1929, when Jack Mitchell, a silver miner, visited them on the way from his mine in Kingman, Arizona, to his home in Los Angeles. He had heard that there were unexplored caves in the mountains, so he and a local rancher rode twenty miles on horseback to the caves. With flashlights, the two men explored as far as the main chamber — enough to motivate Mitchell to immediately stake a claim to this property.

Unfortunately, that was also the year of the stock market crash and the beginning of the Great Depression. Mitchell had to close his unprofitable mine at Kingman. There was no work in Los Angeles, so he and his wife, Ida, left the city in 1934 for the mountains and the caves, which they planned to develop for tourists.

That summer he surveyed and built twenty-two miles of road, and in subsequent years added the stone houses, which are now used at the visitor center and park headquarters. In 1935 the Mitchells built a new trail to the cave entrance and installed stairs and railings in the two caves. They named one "El Pakiva" and the other "Tecopa" for the last Shoshonean chief. Jack Mitchell

Mitchell Caverns

Providence Mountains State Recreation Area
San Bernardino County, California

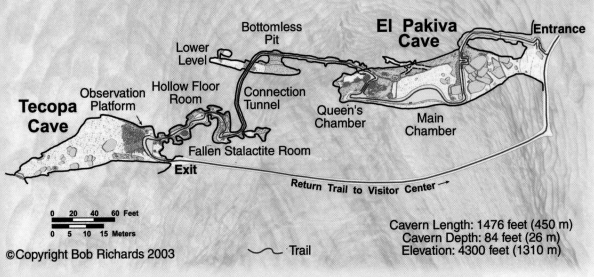

NORTH

Tecopa Cave

Observation Platform

Hollow Floor Room

Lower Level

Bottomless Pit

Connection Tunnel

Fallen Stalactite Room

Exit

El Pakiva Cave

Entrance

Queen's Chamber

Main Chamber

Return Trail to Visitor Center →

0 20 40 60 Feet
0 5 10 15 Meters

~~~ Trail

©Copyright Bob Richards 2003

Cavern Length: 1476 feet (450 m)
Cavern Depth: 84 feet (26 m)
Elevation: 4300 feet (1310 m)

The entrance to El Pakiva Cave

died in 1954, and in 1964 his daughters published his autobiography entitled *Jack Mitchell — Caveman.*

In 1956 the state of California took over the property, installed electric lighting, and, in 1968, connected the two caves with a tunnel. They are now a part of the California Park System.

44

In 1985 Bob Richards led cavers from Los Angeles to survey the cave. The map on page 44, showing 1,476 feet of cave passage, is the result.

THE TOUR

Visitors enter El Pakiva Cave by a 70-foot-long passage and stairs descend to the massively-decorated *Main Chamber*, which is 150 feet long, 50 feet wide, and up to 40 feet high. One wall is covered in flowstone with a profusion of stalactites, stalagmites, and columns. Next is *The Queen's Chamber*, which is also well decorated. Visitors cross *Bottomless Pit* (actually about 30 feet deep) on a bridge before entering the Connection Tunnel.

Once in the second cave, Tecopa, visitors ascend a few steps to *The Fallen Stalactite Room*, which is heavily decorated, as is the next chamber, *The Hollow Floor Room*. The last chamber on the tour is *The Tecopa Room*, which is large and somewhat decorated. Here archeologists have found a femur bone of an Ice Age Ground Sloth. The visitors exit the cave using an entrance enlarged by Jack Mitchell.

TO VISIT

From Interstate 40, about forty-two miles west of Needles and about one hundred miles east of Barstow, take the Essex Road exit and go north for sixteen miles.

In summer the tours are held on the weekends only. In winter, they are offered all week. Phone (760) 928-2586.

Cavern temperature is 65°F. Elevation is 4,300 feet. Tours last about one to 1 1/2 hours (including the hike to the cave) and are limited to twenty-five people.

The Hollow Floor Room

A shield

45

The Main Chamber, spiral staircase, and rappeller

No single word describes Moaning Cavern. *Vast* comes close, as it has the largest chamber of any cave in this book. *Important* would understate its archeological significance. *Thrilling* would describe the long, airy rappel. The spiral staircase is *amazing*. *Fun* sums up *The Adventure Trip*, while formations like *The Igloo* and the sixteen-foot-long stalactite deserve *spectacular*.

HISTORY

Moaning Cave is a prime archeological site because its narrow entrances were traps for unwary animals and humans. Archeologists have found the skeletal remains and artifacts of a tribe of Indians that predate the Miwok.

In about 1850 gold prospectors discovered Moaning Cavern. They lowered themselves to the floor of the main chamber in a large ore-bucket on a winch. With only candles and lamps for light, they searched for gold, but found a mound of dirt and debris containing ancient human skeletons. This prompted the first state geologist of California, John Trask, to investigate the cave in 1851. Trask described the cave's main chamber accurately and then went on to describe three other rooms. His second "room" could be *The Mud Flats*, presently included in *The Adventure Trip*, but his third and fourth rooms have not been located. Since 1920, determined exploration has failed to rediscover Trask's rooms, if they ever existed.

The miners named the cave for the "moaning" sound the cave occasionally emitted. The Miwok Indians, who lived in the area, believed that a stone giant attracted victims by imitating a small child crying. It has since been discovered that under certain conditions, water drops landing in natural, narrow holes in the flowstone at the bottom of the main chamber make a hollow, drumming sound.

The cave was acquired and developed in 1922 by a group of three men — Addison Carley, Dan Malatesta, and Clarence Eltringham. They used dynamite to open a collapsed entrance and installed wooden stairs to bring visitors down sixty-five feet to the top of the main chamber. Albert Tangeman built the one-hundred-foot spiral staircase, now regarded as an architectural feat, without using a single nut or bolt. Instead, the joints were arc-welded. This was the first electric arc welding project west of the Rockies. It

Rappelling

has 144 stairs and spirals seven-and-a-half times. Steve Fairchild, Jr. holds the record for the swiftest ascent of the staircase — an astounding twenty-one seconds.

THE TOUR

The guided tour of Moaning Cavern is very popular and affords excellent views of the cave and rappellers descending 165 feet on ropes.

Anyone over age twelve, one hundred pounds, and four feet tall may do *The Rappel*. Equipment and instruction are provided.

The Adventure Trip, which includes *The Rappel*, takes about three hours. Visitors are supplied with equipment and a guide who leads them through a labyrinth of passages and chambers with names like *Godzilla's Nostril*, *Roach Motel*, and *Black Hole*. This experience is certain to be memorable.

TO VISIT

From Angels Camp go east on Hwy 4 for about six miles, right on Parrotts Ferry Road for about one mile, and then right on Moaning Cave Road. Phone: (209) 736-2708 or (866) 762-2837 www.caverntours.com

Cavern temperature is 59°F. Elevation is 1,700 feet. Tours last about forty-five minutes.

Other attractions include Natural Bridges (pg. 19), Mercer Caverns (pg. 38), water sports on New Melones Reservoir, and historic Columbia.

Handline in Godzilla's Nostril

A multi-level lava tube

Lava Beds National Monument is quite simply the best place in the United States to go lava tubing. With more than five hundred caves in the monument, the opportunities to explore and discover are unlimited and varied. This is one of the few places in the National Park system where the 110,000 visitors each year are encouraged to explore caves on their own! If you need help deciding what to do, talk to a ranger or pick up a guide book, map, or handout at the Visitor Center.

The Monument's Visitor Center is located near *Mushpot Cave*, which has a trail, lights, exhibits, and a theater used for interpretive presentations. The *Cave Loop* area is a two-mile-long road, which accesses seventeen major caves. All are identified with signs and many have improved trails. Exploring this area is an experience that should not be missed. The Monument's longest cave, *The Catacombs*, is on this loop road.

The more isolated caves are well worth visiting. *Valentine Cave* is beautiful and easily explored. *Skull Cave* is impressively huge and has ice. For a more solitary experience, hike the Lyons Trail, which follows a lava tube system for about two miles.

GEOLOGY

The Medicine Lake Volcano produced lava that reached the surface in a very liquid state and flowed for great distances. Thus a low, wide volcano was formed. Though not as tall as most Cascade Range volcanoes (like Mt. Shasta or Mt. Rainier), the Medicine Lake Volcano is by volume and surface area the largest in the range. It is so vast that its discoverers did not recognize it as a volcano, but instead referred to it as a "highland." A lake in the caldera, named Medicine Lake for its reputed healing powers, has lent its name to the volcano. Medicine Lake is at an elevation of 6,676 feet and the surrounding caldera rim rises to 7,913 feet at its highest point.

Lava Beds National Monument is located on the north flank of this volcano and encompasses about ten percent of the Medicine Lake Volcano's surface. Seventy percent of the Monument is covered with lava that erupted thirty to forty thousand years ago.

HOW LAVA TUBES FORM

Lava tubes form when molten magma, with the consistency of hot syrup, erupts and covers the land. Because the lava is intensely hot (1,600 - 1,800° F), the lava stream will build levees along its channel and erode its bed deeper, much like a stream of melted butter poured over an almost level bar of solid butter. This is called *heat erosion*.

Volcanoes often erupt continuously for weeks, months, or even years. The channel may become deeper as more lava flows through it. When the eruption starts to diminish, the top layer of flowing lava cools to form a roof over the channel. As the level of liquid lava drops, the roof gets thicker from splatter. This roof insulates the hot flowing lava from the cool air so the lava can remain molten longer and erode deeper. Superheated gases are trapped in the tube and pressure builds. The tube's interior may "remelt" and smooth molten drips, called "lavacicles," may form. When the eruption stops, part of the remaining lava drains out of the tube, leaving a cave. *Kazamura Cave*, the world's longest known lava tube, on the Big Island of Hawaii, has more than forty miles of surveyed passage. Lava tubes are found in many western states.

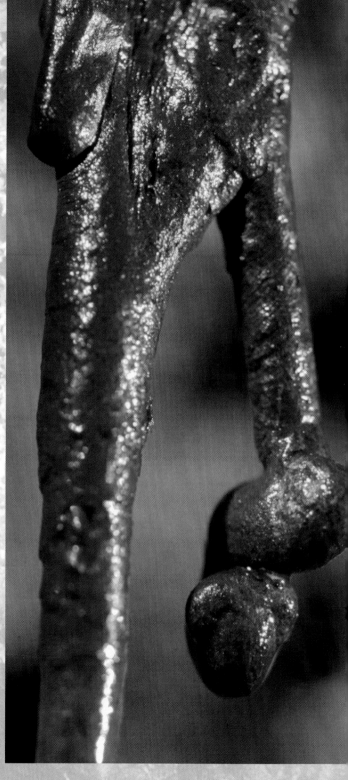

A close-up view of a lavacicle

Valentine Cave

HISTORY

Paleo-Indian cultures lived in the Lava Beds area about 11,500 years ago and successive Indian cultures have used it intensely since then. Today we can see their pictographs in many caves, including *Big Painted Cave* and *Symbol Bridge*. Indians camped at caves having water or ice near the entrance and there is evidence that they used fire to illuminate areas beyond the twilight zone.

Modoc Indians were living in the area when pioneers first arrived in the 1850's and conflicts led to the Modoc Indian War of 1873. An intimate knowledge of the lava fields in this area allowed a band of about fifty Modoc warriors and their families to hold off hundreds of U.S. troops for almost five months.

Homesteaders discovered and named *Bearpaw Cave* in 1888 and *Skull Cave* in about 1892. In 1911 recreational use of the caves began when a road was built to the caves. In 1916, J.D. Howard, a mill worker from Klamath Falls, visited *The Beds*, and for the next twenty years exploration and study of the Medicine Lake volcanic area became his obsession. He discovered and named many of the caves and, with others, produced maps. He is now remembered as *The Father of the Lava Beds*.

In 1920, the "Modoc Lava Beds" became part of the Modoc National Forest and in 1925 became a national monument. The Civilian Conservation Corps (CCC) made infrastructure improvements during the Depression that ended with World War II, including cave trails. 53

CRYSTAL ICE CAVE

How can caves that were formed from molten lava be ideal for accumulating and preserving ice? Lava is not as dense as other rocks, but has air spaces like a sponge, and so it is a good insulator. During winter, cold air sinks into the caves displacing the warmer air. Precipitation seeping through the rocks forms ice upon contact with the freezing air.

Those caves that are relatively deep and have only one entrance at their highest point to reduce air movement are particularly good at forming permanent ice. Some of the shallow, ventilated caves accumulate ice in the winter and spring, but this ice disappears by fall.

THE TOUR

Crystal Ice Cave is about one hundred feet deep and formed on three levels. It has only one entrance and cold air remains in the cave. In order to maintain the outstanding ice speleothems, visits to the cave are limited to twenty trips annually.

Visitors crawl through a gap in the rocks and then descend a ladder. The descent into the cave is steep; the rocks are ice-covered; and although handlines have been installed, care is needed. Most of the trip involves crawling and clambering over rocks. To exit, visitors must use handlines to pull themselves up the icy slope.

To do the tour, visitors must be in good physical condition and have warm clothes, gloves, helmet, and sturdy shoes. Each visitor should have a headlamp and spare flashlights. Children must be at least twelve years old and accompanied by an adult. Rangers guide six-person tours on Saturdays from December 1 through March 31 at about 1 p.m. The tour lasts about 2 1/2 hours. Reservations must be made no more than three weeks in advance by phoning the Lava Beds Visitor Center at (530) 667-2282, and pressing 1.

Skull Cave

SAFETY AND CONSERVATION

As you enjoy the freedom to move through these lava tubes, avoid damaging the caves and do not place yourself or others at risk. Make sure that you and each person in your group has his/her own battery-powered light and spare batteries. Headlamps are best because hands are then free for balancing. Anything with a flame is prohibited. Wear a helmet for head protection. If you do not have a helmet or light, drop by the Visitor Center to borrow a light and buy an inexpensive bump cap.

Stay on the trails and keep away from unstable areas. Do not run or jump. Keep your party together. Bring layers of warm clothes and wear sturdy shoes. No glass may be taken into the caves. Smoking is prohibited in all National Park caves.

You must never deface the caves or leave litter. There are no bathrooms in the caves, so you should use the facilities at the Visitor Center.

TO VISIT

Lava Beds is located midway between San Francisco and Portland, Oregon. Exit Interstate 5 at Weed. Proceed northeast on Highway 97 through Dorris to the Oregon border, then east seventeen miles on Highway 161, then south at the sign to the Monument. Phone (530) 667-2282.

Cavern temperatures vary, typically around 50°F. Elevation is 4,791 feet.

Other attractions include the National Wildlife Refuges, Captain Jack's Stronghold, Glass Mountain, and water sports at Medicine Lake.

SUBWAY CAVE

This lava tube looks like a subway tunnel with a ceiling height of six to seventeen feet, and with a reasonably smooth floor. It is the longest cave in the twenty-thousand-year-old Hat Creek lava flow and is important in local Indian mythology.

TO VISIT

The cave is located near the town of Old Station and opposite Cave Campground, a quarter mile north of the junction of Highways 44 and 89. Visit the Forest Service Old Station Information Center. Phone (530) 336-5521 or 335-7517. Cavern temperature is 46°F. Elevation is 4,330 feet.

Settlers discovered the cave about 1884. The United States Forest Service has gradually developed the cave since 1905; by 1920 it was a major tourist attraction. Teams of cavers led by J.R. Evans in 1962 and Liz Wolff in 1985 mapped the cave.

From May through October, the cave is open to visitors who must bring their own headlamps and helmets to view the impressive tube's interior. There are three thousand feet of passage in the cave, about half of which are open to visitors. There are trails leading to the entrances, stairways leading down in the cave, and interpretive signs describing lava cave features.

PLUTO'S CAVE

Pluto's Cave is a large tube in lava, which flowed about 160,000 years ago. It was discovered in 1863 by a rancher, Nelson Cash, while he was looking for stray cattle. Cash named it for the Roman god of the underworld.

John Muir, who visited the cave prior to 1888, saw the heads and horns of many wild sheep near Indian campfires at the entrance.

In 1983 Peter Bosted led a team of cavers to survey the main part of the cave to a length of 2,500 feet. In 1996 the land surrounding the cave was acquired by the Klamath National Forest, which is responsible for conserving the physical and biological integrity of the cave. A brochure on the cave is available from the Forest Service office in Macdoel.

The first half of the cave is sandy-floored, while the second half has large rocks on the floor and high ceilings. The final two hundred feet is a narrow crawl. Bring your own helmet and headlamp. The safety and conservation guidelines on page 56 apply to this cave.

TO VISIT

From Highway 97, twelve miles north of Weed and forty-two miles south of Dorris, turn onto Country Road A-12. After 3.1 miles turn left on a dirt road beside a Forest Service sign. Temperatures vary. Elevation about 3,380 feet.

SUNNY JIM CAVE

The *Seven Sisters of La Jolla* are among the most notable sea caves on the California coast. The best known of these is Sunny Jim Cave, so named because the cave's entrance resembles the profile of a cartoon character from the 1920's.

TO VISIT

From Interstate 5, exit at La Jolla Village. Drive and turn right. After 0.7 miles, turn left on Torrey Pines Drive and proceed for nearly two miles. Follow signs to La Jolla Cave. The cave is open daily 9-5. Phone (858) 459-0746. Other attractions include sea kayaking to the Seven Sisters (858) 459-1114.

Since 1903 visitors have been able to enter this cave through a tunnel built by laborers hired by a German professor, Gustav Schultz. Today, people descend the 144 stairs to enjoy the sound of barking sea lions, cooing pigeons, and breaking waves from a wooden viewing platform. The main chamber is nearly one hundred feet long and forty feet high.

Pacific Ocean waves have eroded *The Sisters* from horizontally layered sandstone containing thin layers of shale, mudstone, and conglomerates. Fossils can be found in the shales and mudstones. These sedimentary rocks are between 89 and 121 million years old.

Balconies Cave is quite different from the preceeding carbonate, lava, and sea caves, largely because of its unusual genesis. It is located in Pinnacles National Monument, which is a group of jutting spires standing on a high ridge east of Soledad. These spires are all that remain of half a volcano. The other half is near Lancaster, northeast of Los Angeles.

The volcano originally formed on a fault in the San Andreas rift zone some twenty-three million years ago. The fault occurred as a result of slow motion along the boundary between the North American Plate and the Pacific Plate. Molten magma rose along cracks and faults adjacent to the San Andreas Fault, forming the volcano of pasty rhyolite volcanic rock. Over time, the San Andreas Fault slowly tore the volcano in half, transporting the western half nearly two hundred miles to the north to its present site near Hollister.

Wind, water, and ice eroded deep canyons into the rock along vertical cracks, slowly reducing its size and strength. As the blocky towers weathered, they either slowly slid down into the narrow canyons or were suddenly toppled by large earthquakes along the adjacent San Andreas Fault. Today, these former tower tops appear as boulders and the canyons, which they now roof, are called *talus caves* . Bruce Rogers surveyed Balconies Cave to a length of 576 feet in 1997.

Severe flooding during extremely wet *El Niño* years rearranges the smaller, loose rocks inside the cave, making the cave trail a constant "work in progress." The cave may be closed after winter storms. Most of the water dries up during the hot summers, but a few seeps continue to run year-round, providing water for reclusive animals.

Balconies Cave is the most popular destination in the Monument and attracts tens of thousands of visitors each year. The Monument's other cave, Bear Gulch Cave, is closed for about eleven months each year to protect the bats. Visitors need to bring their own helmet and headlamp. Kneepads add extra comfort.

TO VISIT

Take Highway 101 to Soledad and follow the signs for Pinnacles National Monument through the town and along route 146 for twelve miles. Phone (831) 389-4485. www.nps.gov/pinn

Cave temperatures vary from low sixties in summer to freezing in winter. Elevation is 1,345 feet.

Other attractions include Paraiso Hot Springs, wine tasting, Arroyo Seco, and rock-climbing.

BEYOND CALIFORNIA

Most states have caves to visit. For more information, contact the National Caves Association (NCA) by calling toll free 1-866-55-CAVES to request a free copy of their *Cave Directory*. This shows at a glance where almost one hundred caves are located and how to contact the caves. The best concentrations of caves to visit are in the Shenandoah Valley, Kentucky, Indiana, and the Ozarks.

Carlsbad Caverns in southeast New Mexico is a "must." It has one of the world's largest cave chambers, which has to be seen to be believed. Here, visitors can stroll through magnificent chambers at their own pace. Allow two to five hours for this unique experience.

Visitors can also join guided tours, which can be reserved in advance by calling 1-800-967-2283. *The Kings Palace Tour* and the *Left Hand Tunnel Tour* are very popular, while those who like wild caving (crawling, ladders, ropes) should ask about *Lower Cave*, *Hall of the White Giants*, and *Spider Cave*. *Slaughter Canyon Cave* is great for visitors who like to explore with their own lights.

Slaughter Canyon Cave entrance

ACKNOWLEDGMENTS

We could not have produced this book without the expert contributions from many talented, knowledgeable, and helpful people who willingly assisted in countless ways.

Our sincere thanks go to Steve and John Fairchild, Roger LeFebvre, and Steve Rawlings for their support and encouragement. Ray Miller was our editor, while Lisa Boulton, John Fairchild, Dr. Jerald Johnson, Bruce Rogers, and Dan Snyder scrutinized many of the chapters and offered useful suggestions. Jim Borden, Pat Helton, and Howard Hurtt proofread. Dan Clardy was our most frequent photo assistant.

Scott Rule earned our gratitude for his stunning layout, endless patience, and dedication. We are indebted to Bob Richards, Bruce Rogers, and Mike & Lynne Sims for allowing us to use their fine cave maps. Thanks also to Dave and Carol Belski, Molly Bosted, Chuck Chavdarian, Toinette Hartshorne, Cindy Heazlit, Iris Heusler, Tom and Mary McAfee, Annette McGarr, Ray Miller, Irmgild Schack, and Gary and Jenny Whitby for making the final photo selection.

We thank Rich Wolfert and Rick Rhinehart for suggesting the project, Barbara Bolton for managing it, Carl Tootle for his friendly advice, and Alpha CD Imaging for scanning our photos.

We sincerely thank the following for their contributions, listed by chapter.

History. Reviewed by Dr. Michael Moratto.

Geology. Reviewed by Dr. Marek Cichanski, Dr. Bradley Hacker, Dr. Carol Ann Hill, and Greg Stock.

Speleothems. Reviewed by Dr. Carol Ann Hill. Photo assistants: Dave Bunnell and Don Coons.

Black Chasm. Reviewed by Greg and Shaundy Francek. Photo assistants: Dave Cowan, Trevor Carter, Greg Francek, Toinette Hartshorne, Cindy Heazlit, Chris Mitracos, Rachel Smith, and Lynn Van Erden.

Boyden Cavern. Reviewed by John Scott-Lamb. Photo assistants: Jeff Butt, Mick Fingleton, Jason & Jeaninne Scott-Lamb.

Calaveras Natural Bridges. Reviewed by Joshua Feinberg. Photo assistants: James de la Loza, Francois Hughes, and Peter McAfee.

California Cavern. Reviewed by Art Holley. Photo assistants (including cover photo, pages 4 and 9): Danny Anderson, Jacques & Marie-Ange Chabert, Eli Fairchild, Toinette Hartshorne, Damien Ivereigh, Glen Malliet, Chris Mitracos, Rene Scherer and Rachel Smith.

Map surveyors: Bob Baker, John Fairchild, Paul Greaves, Charmaine Leggé, Paul Lukshin, Gary Mele, B. Pine, Bruce Rogers, Ralph Squire, and Eric Tsakle.

Crystal Cave. Reviewed by Abby Snow. Photo assistants (including page 7): Hazel Barton, Kip Baumann, Tim McCoy, Steve and Matt Ruble, Scott Schmidt, Lynn Van Erden, and Marguerite and Helen Williams.
Map surveyors: Kyle Bentley, Rich Breisch, Marc Boillat, Royce and Ronna Chezem, Greg Cotterman, Phil Darling, Joel Despain, David Engel, Charlie Festerson, Bill Frantz, Steve and Mary Koehler, Dale and Kathy Lankford, Paul Lukshin, Glen Malliet, Paul Nelson, Vance Nelson, Brent Ort, Randy Pipp, Bob Richards, Steve and Barbara Ruble, Lori Schultz, Vern Smith, and Carol Vesley.

Lake Shasta Caverns. Reviewed by Roger Le Febvre. Photo assistants: Nelson de la Loza, Damian, Amanda and Damon Grindley, Dick La Forge, Ray Miller, Jock, Marguerite, Helen and David Williams, and Liz Wolff.
Map surveyors: Lynne and Mike Sims, Tim Anderson, Dian Anderson, Dell Talent, Steve Johnson, Bernie Dunn, and Tom Houck.

Mercer Caverns. Reviewed by Bernard Ingram and Steve Rawlings. Photo assistants: Annette McGarr, Tim Hughes, and Fiona Bradfield.
Map surveyors: Bruce Rogers, Charmaine Leggé, and Paul Decker.
Book quotes: Dr. William R. Halliday, *Caves of California* (1962)

Mitchell Caverns. Reviewed by Myke Ray and Bob Richards. Photo assistants: Jeff Cheraz, Bill and Brian Farr, Tom Kaylor, Jed Mosenfelder, Carol Vesley, and Fumie Yamaguchi.
Map surveyors: Bob Richards, Carol Conroy, and Don and Lisa DeLucia.

Moaning Cavern. Photo assistants: Kristen Ankiewicz, Jeff Cheraz, Steve Fairchild, Tim Hughes, Mark Scott, and Lisa Tesler.

Lava Beds NM. Reviewed by Dr. Julie Donnelly-Nolan, Craig Dorman, Kelly Fuhrmann, Cecilia Mitchell, and Matt Reece. Photo assistants: James de la Loza, Terry de Silva, Kelly Fuhrmann, Toinette Hartshorne, Iris Heusler, Ray Miller, and James Wilson.

Pluto's Cave. Reviewed by Bill Broekel, Dr. Robert Christiansen, and Juan de la Fuente. Photo assistant (including photo below): Ray Miller.

Sunny Jim Cave. Reviewed by Bob Richards. Photo assistant: James de la Loza.

Beyond California. Photo assistants: Djuna Bewley, Tim Jones, and Dick DesJardins.

— Peter and Ann Bosted

Pluto's Cave.